P
597.8
-STO-

Y0-DLE-968

North Smithfield Public Library
Slatersville, RI

TOADS

NIGHTTIME ANIMALS

35931 – Jan. 1995

Lynn M. Stone

The Rourke Corporation, Inc.
Vero Beach, Florida 32964

© 1993 The Rourke Corporation, Inc.

All rights reserved. No part of this book may be reproduced or utilized in any form or by any means, electronic or mechanical including photocopying, recording or by any information storage and retrieval system without permission in writing from the publisher.

Edited by Sandra A. Robinson

PHOTO CREDITS
All photos © Lynn M. Stone except pages 7, 10 and 13 © Breck Kent

Library of Congress Cataloging-in-Publication Data

Stone, Lynn M.
  Toads / by Lynn M. Stone.
    p. cm. — (Nighttime animals)
  Includes index.
  Summary: Discusses the habitats, physical characteristics, habits, predators, and prey of different kinds of toads.
    ISBN 0-86593-294-8
    1. Toads—Juvenile literature. [1. Toads.] I. Title. II. Series: Stone, Lynn M. Nighttime animals.
QL688.E227S76 1993
597.8'7—dc20   93-15696
                                              CIP
                                              AC

3 5944 00035 9313

TABLE OF CONTENTS

Toads	5
Where Toads Live	6
How Toads Look	9
Kinds of Toads	11
Toad Cousins	14
Toad Habits	16
Predators and Prey	19
From Egg to Adult	20
Toads and People	22
Glossary	23
Index	24

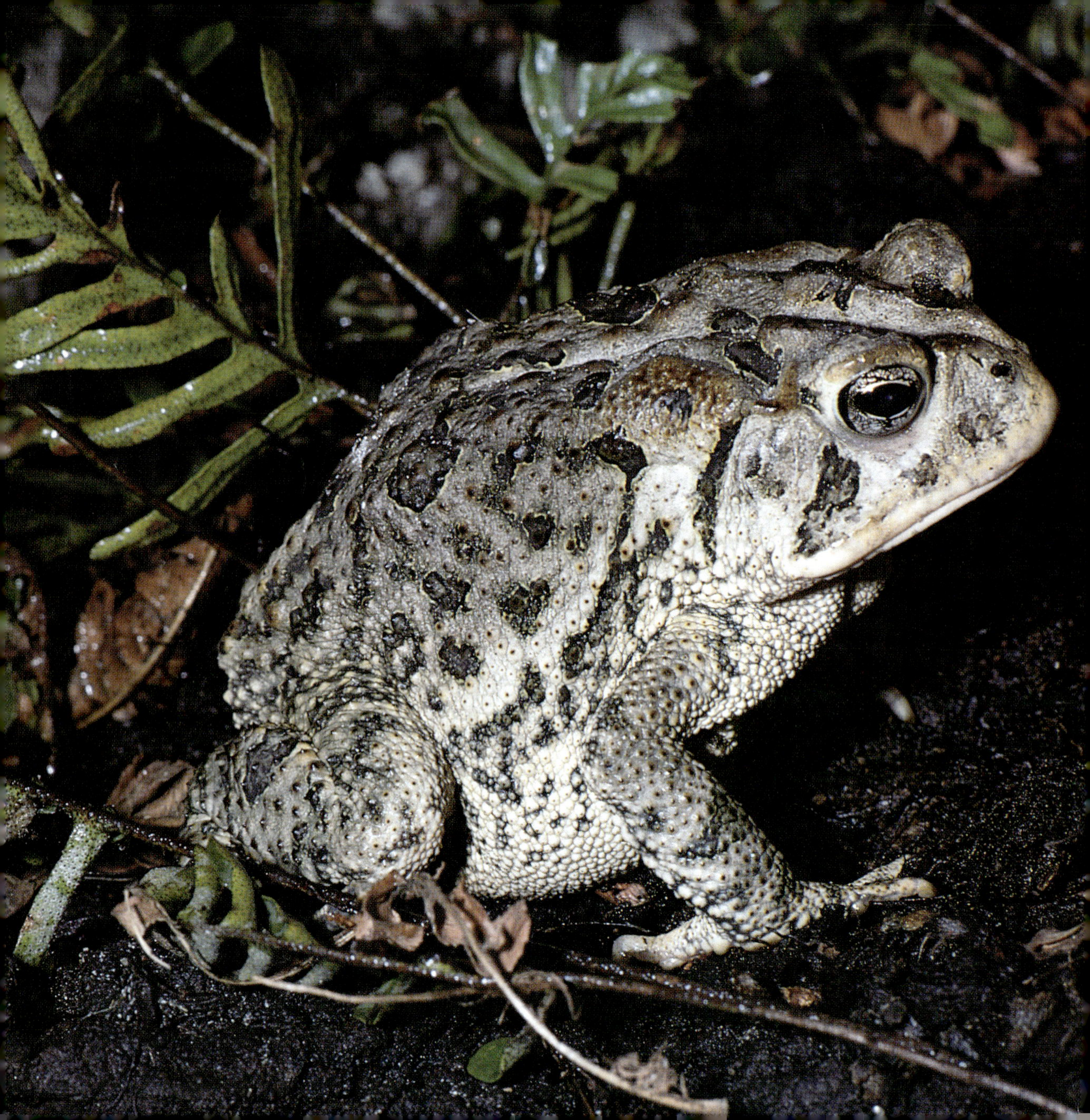

TOADS

Toads are soft, warty **amphibians.** Toads are closely related to frogs.

Toads generally hide and rest during the day, but they are active at night, or **nocturnal.** Because they are nocturnal, toads avoid many **predators**—animals that would like to eat them.

Toads are not leapers. They hop from place to place and have earned the nickname "hoptoad."

The southern toad and its cousins are creatures of the night

WHERE TOADS LIVE

Toads live in many different **habitats,** or types of land. Most toad habitats are in warm, wet areas. Some kinds, or **species,** live in the high South American Andes. Other species live in deserts.

Toads live on all of the continents except Australia and Antarctica. They live throughout North America except in the frozen Far North.

The western spadefoot toad lives in dry areas of the West

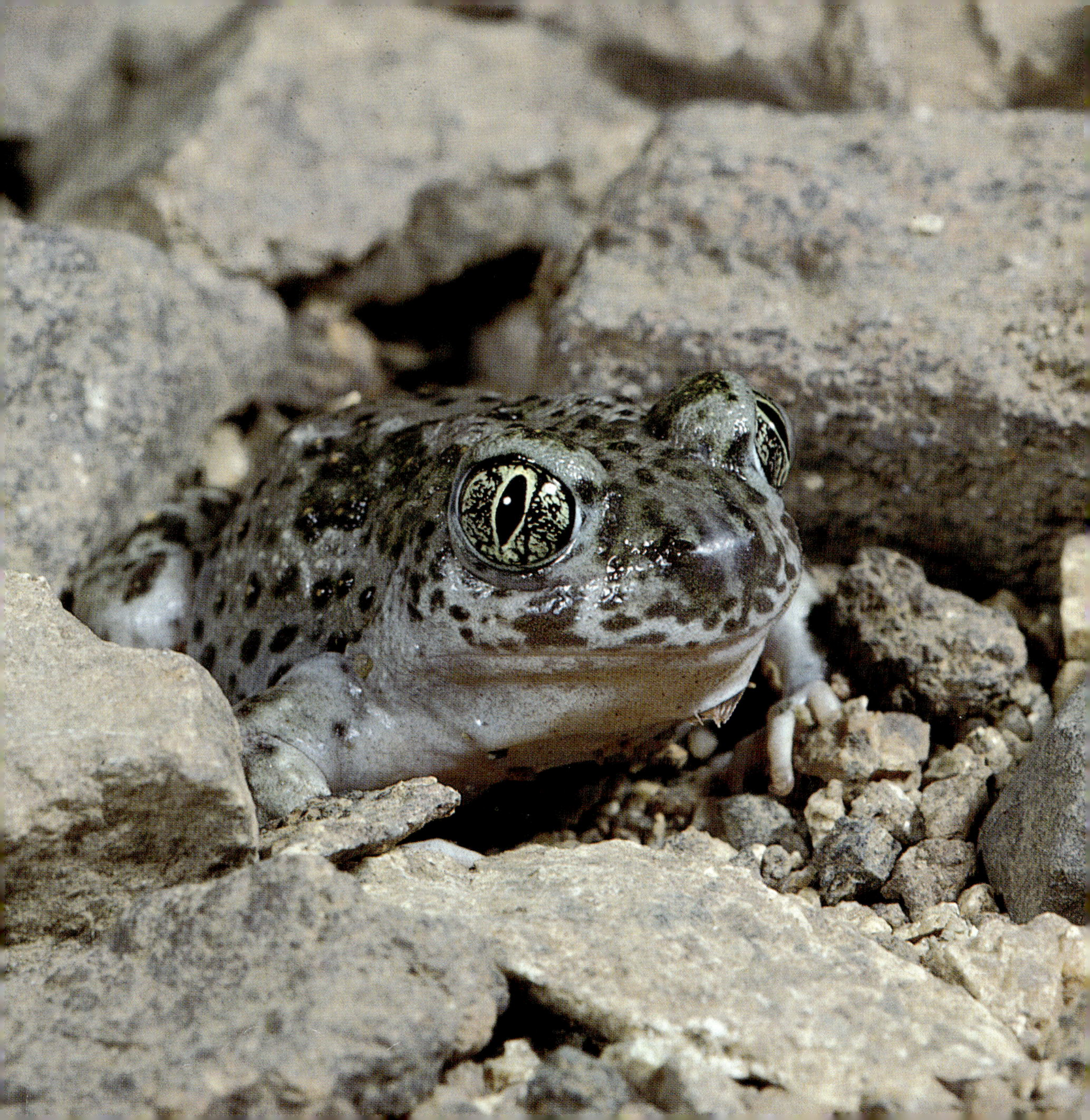

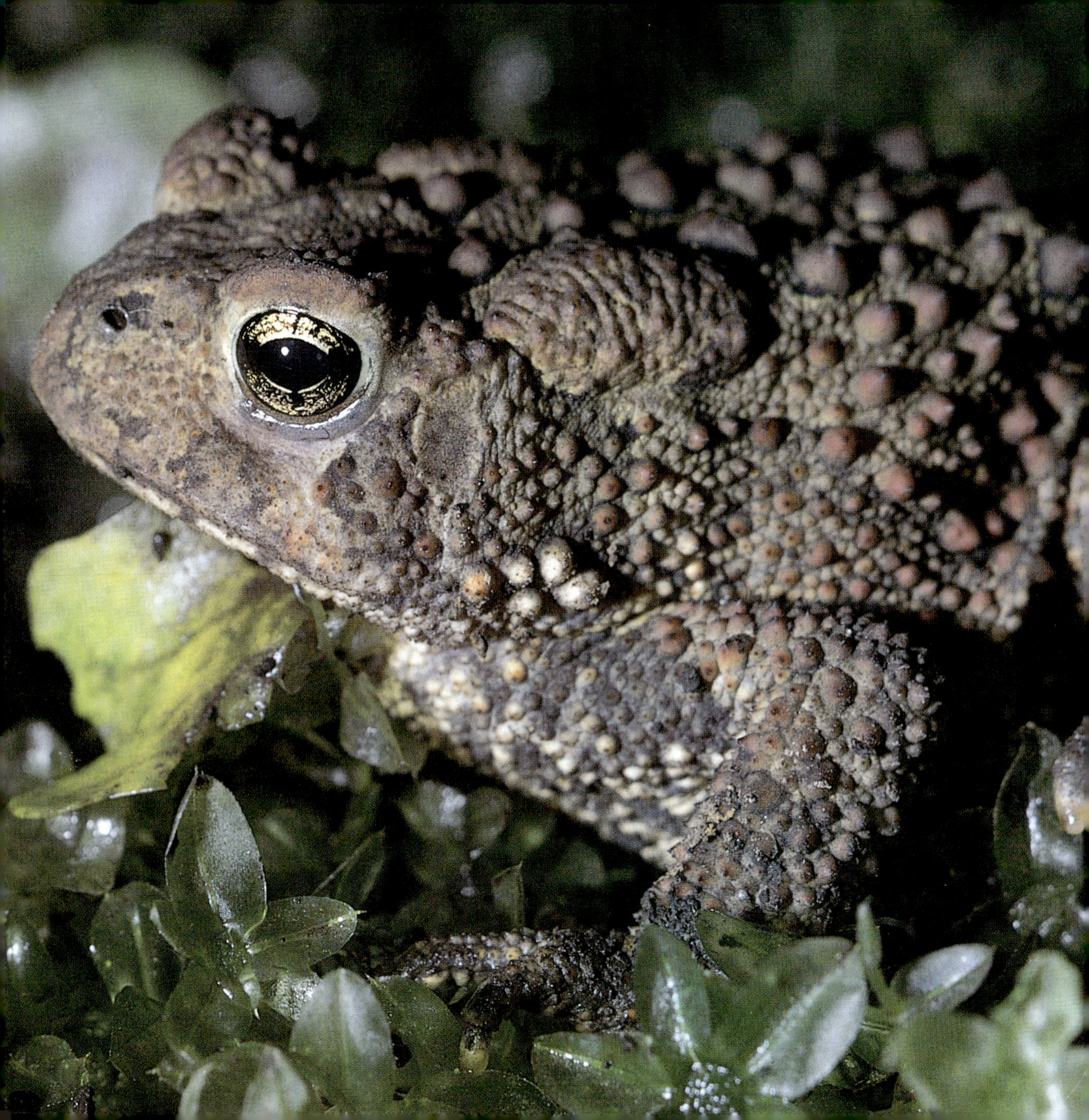

HOW TOADS LOOK

Most toads have lumpy, or warty, skin. The skin is usually a shade of gray, brown or olive, or a mixture of those colors. Dull coloring helps toads **camouflage** themselves, or blend in with their surroundings.

Spadefoot toads are unusual. They have a sharp-edged "spade" on each hind foot for digging, and catlike eyes.

The giant toad of South America is the world's largest. One was nearly 10 inches long.

The toad's earth-colored skin is warty

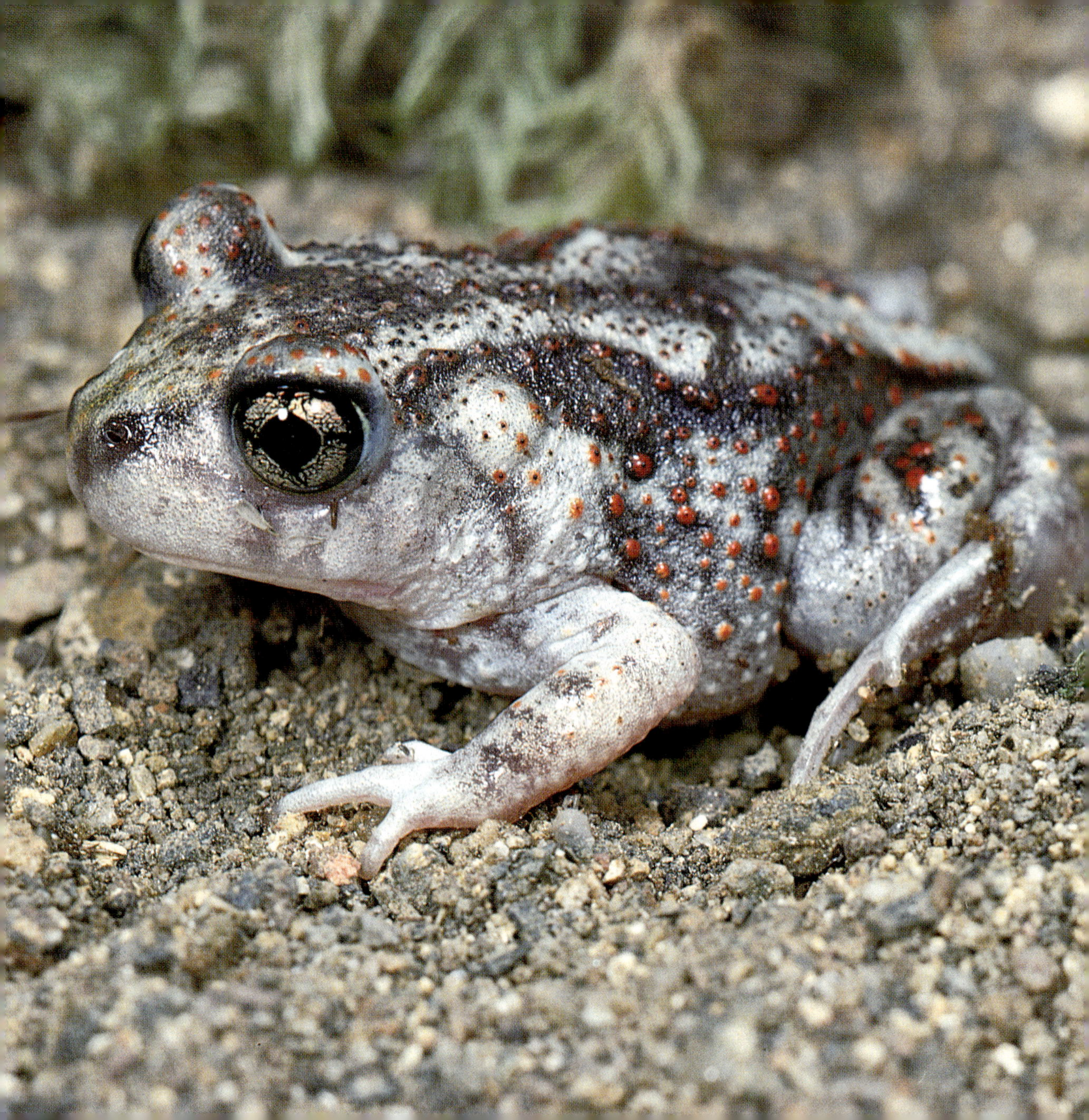

KINDS OF TOADS

Most toads in North America are in one of two groups: "true" toads and spadefoot toads. The American toad, one of the common "hoptoads," and its cousins are "true" toads. Spadefoot toads are toads that dig.

Toads differ in size and color. They also differ in the way their toes are made, the warts on their skin, and in other ways.

The eastern spadefoot, shown here, and other spadefoot toads burrow

An American toad sizes up dinner, a night crawler

A great basin spadefoot toad burrowed in Oregon sand

TOAD COUSINS

As an amphibian, a toad is related to frogs and salamanders. All of these soft, moist-skinned animals are born in the water. Most of them, however, live on land as adults.

Frogs generally spend more time around water than toads. Frogs have smoother skin than toads, and they leap rather than hop.

Other amphibians are something like frogs and something like toads.

The smooth-skinned frogs spend more time in and around water than toads do

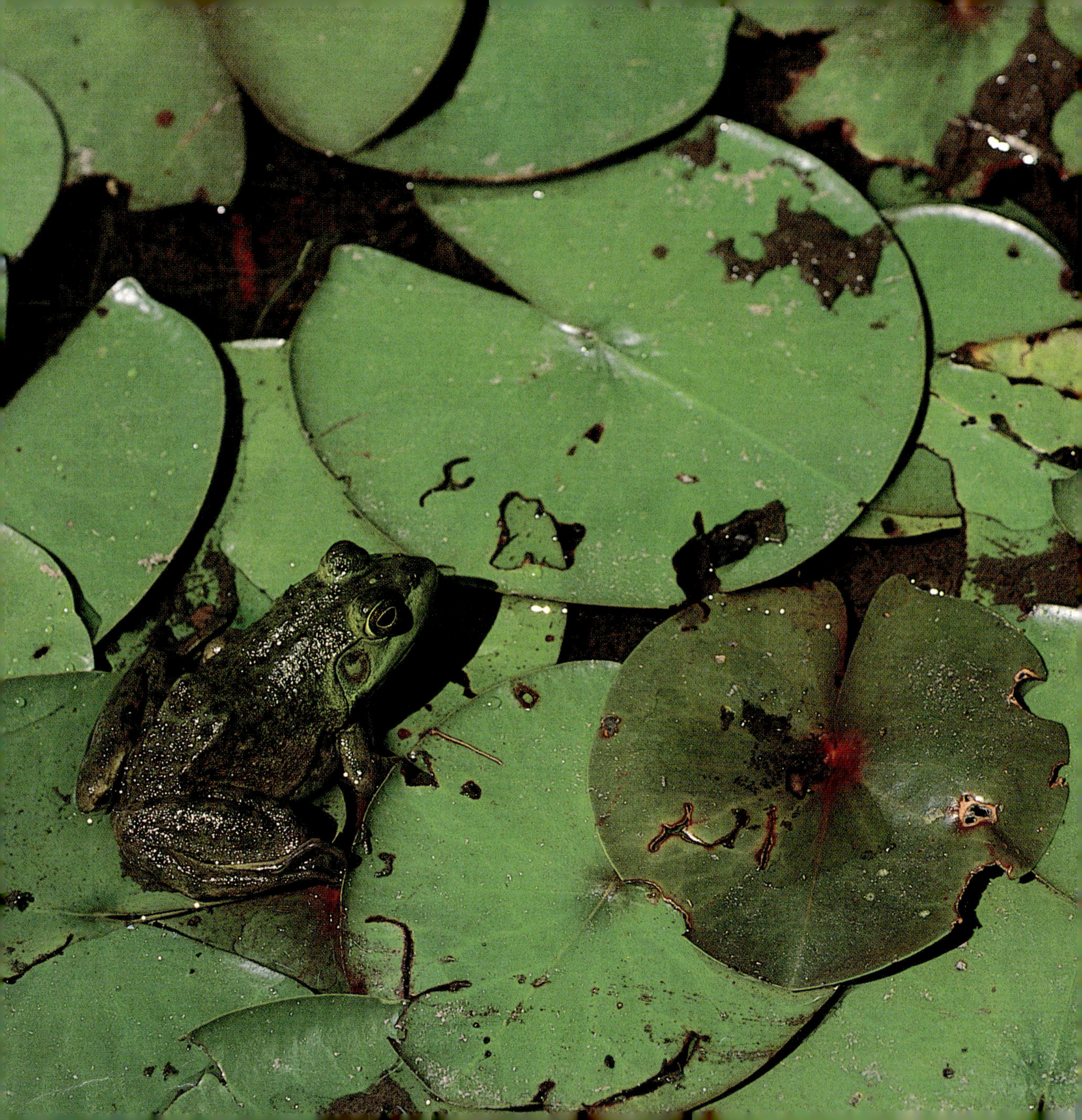

TOAD HABITS

Toads in desert areas stay in underground burrows until it rains. Toads in the North spend winters underground. They come out when warm weather returns.

Male toads call loudly to attract mates. They call by filling a **vocal sac** with air. In the North, their loud trilling is one of the sure signs and sounds of spring. In the South, male toads may call on almost any warm, rainy night.

With its vocal sac puffed up, an American toad welcomes spring and woos a mate

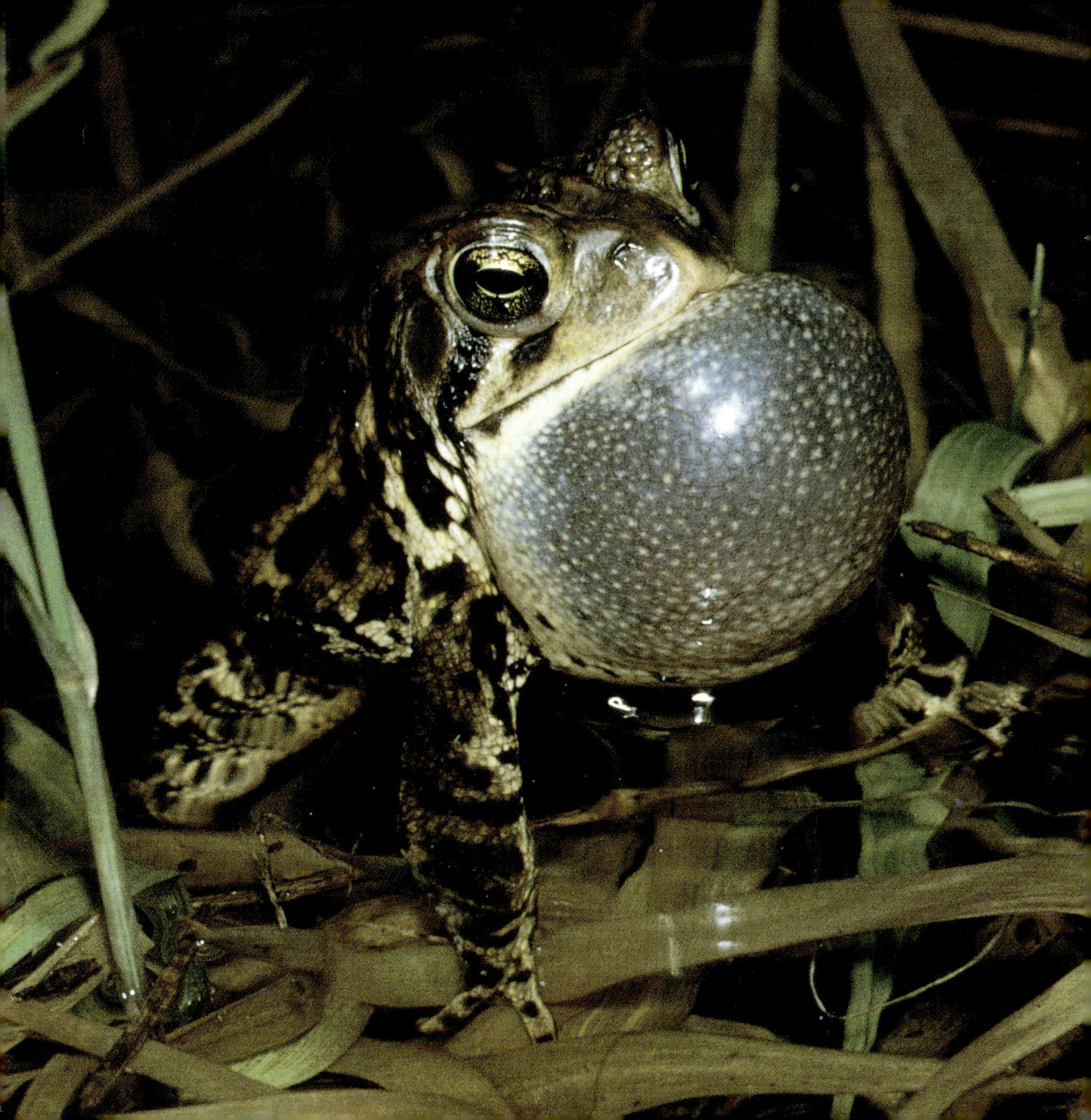

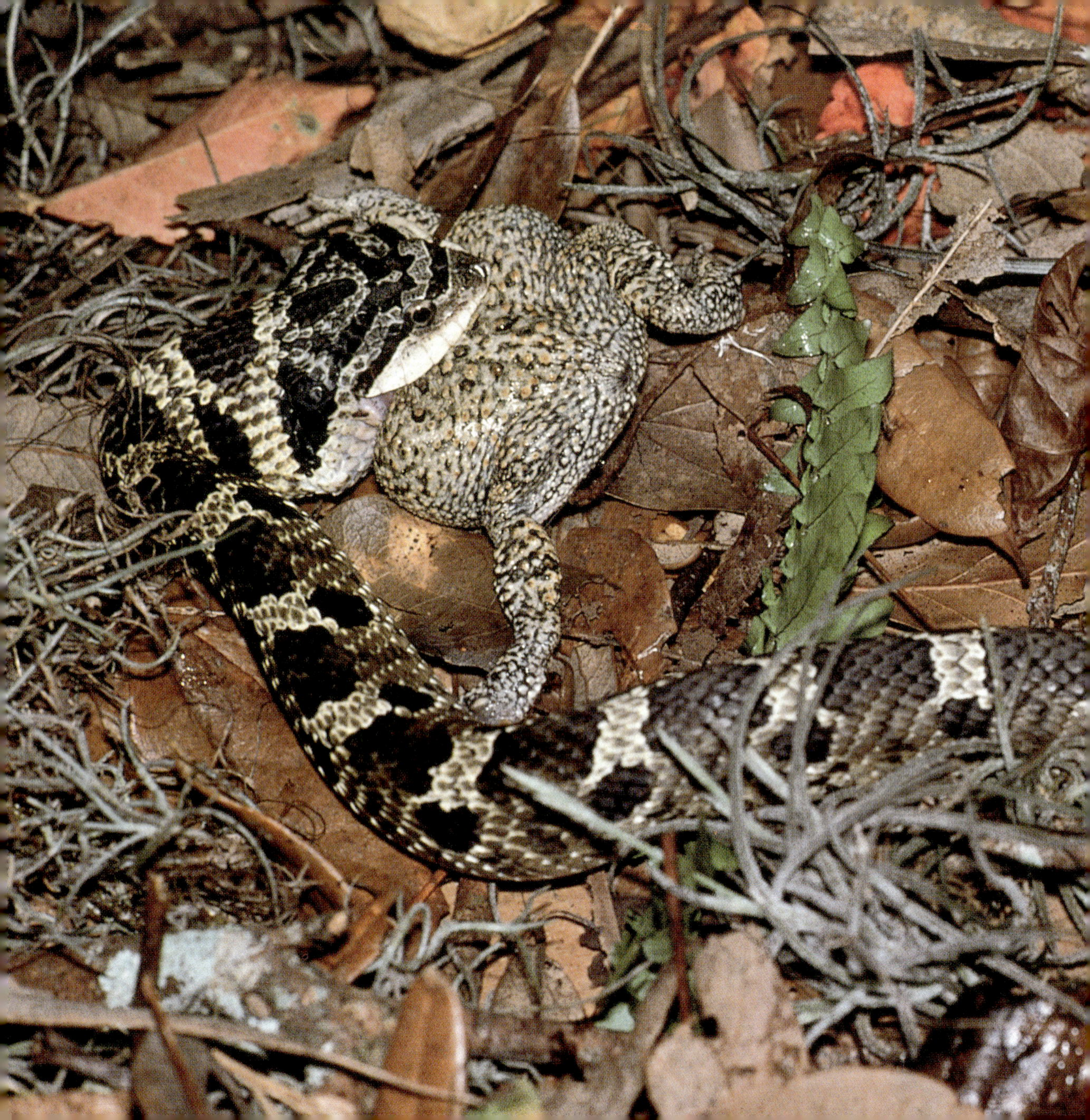

PREDATORS AND PREY

Toads are predators, or hunters, because they eat other animals. Most of their **prey**—the animals they catch—are insects. Toads also eat slugs, worms, snails and other small, boneless creatures.

Toads are excited by the movement of prey. Most toads grab their prey by flipping out their long, sticky tongues.

Toads themselves become prey for many larger predators, including the hognosed snake, which eats nothing but toads!

A southern toad is prey to a hognosed snake

FROM EGG TO ADULT

Female toads lay jellylike strings of eggs in ponds, marshes and standing pools of rainwater.

The tiny **tadpoles** that hatch look like fish. They have no legs, but they have a wriggly tail and breathe underwater like fish.

Tadpoles grow rapidly and sprout legs. Later, a young toad leaves the water. It loses its tail and becomes an air-breathing adult toad.

Fishlike toad tadpoles will later sprout legs, lose their tail and climb onto land

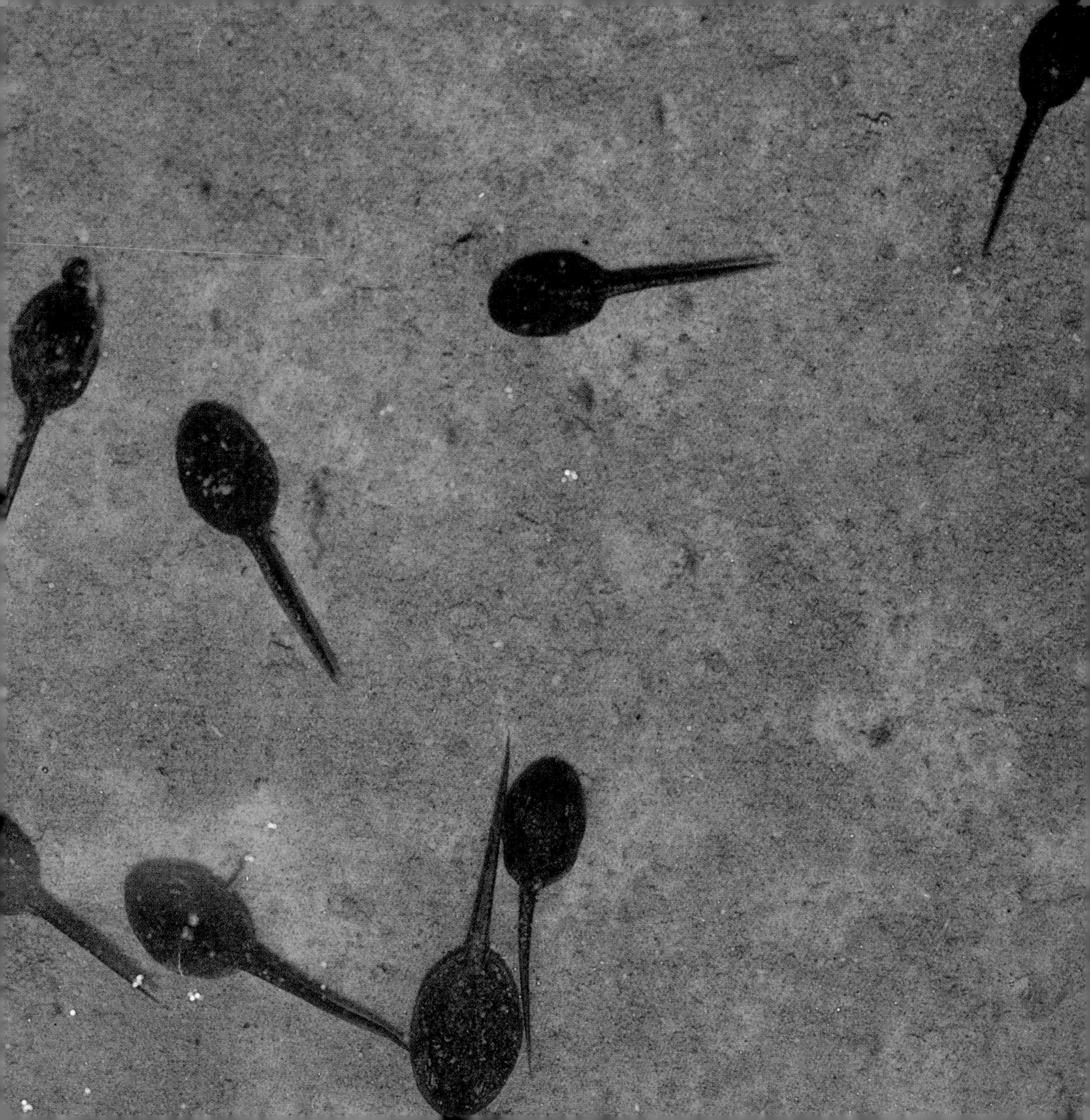

TOADS AND PEOPLE

People generally like toads because these animals eat many insects. A few people believe that toads cause warts. Toads' skin does produce a liquid that may irritate human skin, but toads do not cause warts.

The Houston toad and the Wyoming toad are **endangered.** They are in danger of disappearing—becoming **extinct**—because many of their habitats have been replaced by buildings.

Glossary

amphibian (am FIB ee en) — any of a group of soft animals with backbones that are born in water, but, in most cases, become air-breathing as adults; frogs, toads and salamanders

camouflage (KAM o flahj) — to hide by matching an animal's color to its surroundings

endangered (en DANE jerd) — in danger of no longer existing; very rare

extinct (ex TINKT) — the point at which an animal species no longer exists

habitat (HAB uh tat) — the kind of place in which an animal lives, such as swampland

nocturnal (nahk TUR nul) — active at night

predator (PRED uh tor) — an animal that kills other animals for food

prey (PRAY) — an animal that is hunted for food by another animal

species (SPEE sheez) — within a group of closely-related living things, one certain kind or type (*American* toad)

tadpole (TAD pole) — young frogs and toads while they still live in water

vocal sac (VO kul SAHK) — a balloonlike structure that can be filled with air to produce sound

INDEX

amphibians 5, 14
burrows 16
colors 9, 11
deserts 6
eggs 20
eyes 9
foot 9
frogs 5, 14
habitats 6, 22
insects 19, 22
legs 20
night 5, 16
North America 6, 11
people 22
predators 5, 19
prey 19
salamanders 14
size 11
skin 9, 11, 22

snake, hognosed 19
spring 16
tadpoles 20
tail 20
toad
  American 11
  giant 9
  Houston 22
  spadefoot 9, 11
  "true" 11
  Wyoming 22
toes 11
tongues 19
trilling 16
vocal sac 16
warts 22
winters 16

NORTH SMITHFIELD PUBLIC LIBRARY

3 5944 00035 9313

JAN -- 1995

DATE DUE			
NOV 25 1995			
MAY 4 1996			
25 MAY 1996			
AUG 30 1996			
26 FEB 1997			
24 JUN 1997			
7 AUG 1997			
OCT 03 1997			
SEP 10 1998			

NORTH SMITHFIELD PUBLIC LIBRARY
20 MAIN STREET P.O. BOX 950
SLATERSVILLE, RI 02876